HAL•LEONARD
INSTRUMENTAL PLAY-ALONG

AUDIO ACCESS INCLUDED

PLAYBACK+
Speed • Pitch • Balance • Loop

ALTO SAX

IRIS FAVORITES

CONTENTS

To access audio visit:
www.halleonard.com/mylibrary
Enter Code
6215-5134-5816-5679

ISBN 978-1-4234-9526-0

HAL•LEONARD®

Visit Hal Leonard Online at
www.halleonard.com

Contact us:
Hal Leonard
7777 West Bluemound Road
Milwaukee, WI 53213
Email: info@halleonard.com

In Europe, contact:
Hal Leonard Europe Limited
42 Wigmore Street
Marylebone, London, W1U 2RN
Email: info@halleonardeurope.com

In Australia, contact:
Hal Leonard Australia Pty. Ltd.
4 Lentara Court
Cheltenham, Victoria, 3192 Australia
Email: info@halleonard.com.au

BELIEVE ME, IF ALL THOSE
ENDEARING YOUNG CHARMS

ALTO SAX

Words and Music by
THOMAS MOORE

THE BELLS OF ST. MARY'S

ALTO SAX

Words by DOUGLAS FURBER
Music by A. EMMETT ADAMS

BLACK VELVET BAND

ALTO SAX

Traditional

BRENNAN ON THE MOOR

ALTO SAX

Traditional

COCKLES AND MUSSELS
(Molly Malone)

ALTO SAX

Traditional

THE CROPPY BOY

ALTO SAX

18th Century Irish Folksong

DANNY BOY

Words by FREDERICK EDWARD WEATHERLY
Traditional Irish Folk Melody

ALTO SAX

EASY AND SLOW

ALTO SAX

Traditional

THE FOGGY DEW

ALTO SAX

Traditional

GREEN GROW THE RUSHES, O

ALTO SAX

Traditional

THE HUMOUR IS ON ME NOW

ALTO SAX

Traditional

I ONCE LOVED A LASS

ALTO SAX

Traditional

I'LL TAKE YOU HOME AGAIN, KATHLEEN

ALTO SAX

Words and Music by
THOMAS WESTENDORF

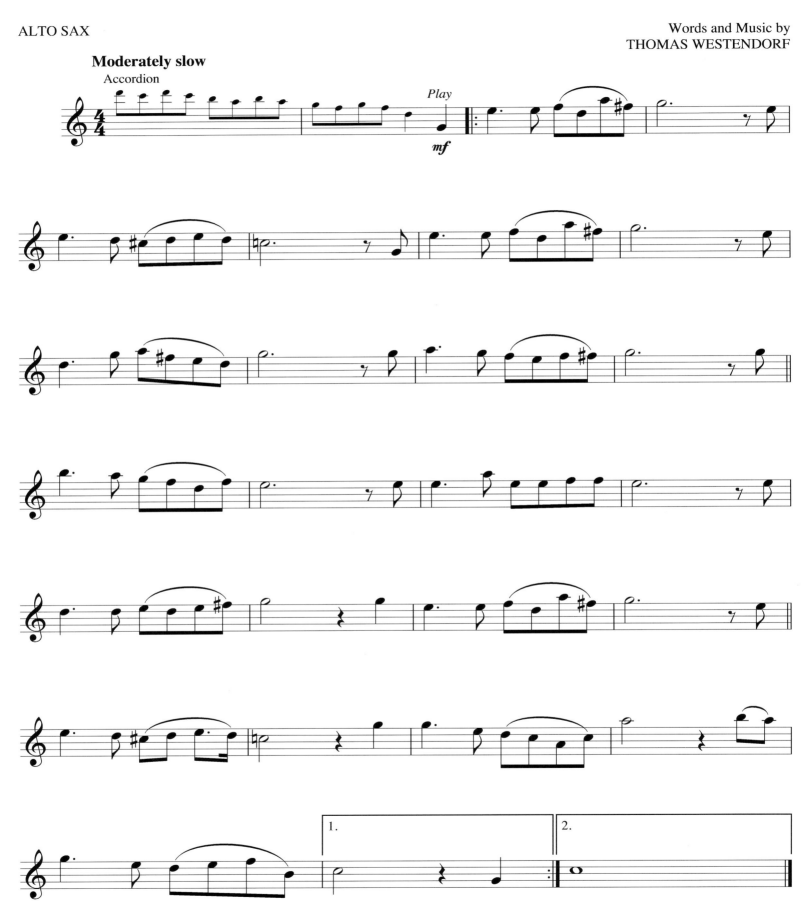

I'LL TELL ME MA

ALTO SAX

Traditional

THE IRISH ROVER

ALTO SAX

Traditional

THE JOLLY BEGGARMAN

ALTO SAX

Traditional

THE LITTLE BEGGARMAN

ALTO SAX

Traditional

MacNAMARA'S BAND

ALTO SAX

Words by JOHN J. STAMFORD
Music by SHAMUS O'CONNOR

MINSTREL BOY

ALTO SAX

Traditional

MY WILD IRISH ROSE

ALTO SAX

Words and Music by
CHAUNCEY OLCOTT

A NATION ONCE AGAIN

ALTO SAX

Words and Music by
THOMAS DAVIS

THE OLD ORANGE FLUTE

ALTO SAX

Traditional

THE PATRIOT GAME

ALTO SAX

Traditional

RED IS THE ROSE

ALTO SAX

Irish Folksong

THE RISING OF THE MOON

ALTO SAX

Traditional

THE ROSE OF TRALEE

ALTO SAX

Words by C. MORDAUNT SPENCER
Music by CHARLES W. GLOVER

TOO-RA-LOO-RA-LOO-RAL
(That's an Irish Lullabye)

ALTO SAX

Words and Music by
JAMES R. SHANNON

THE WEARING OF THE GREEN

ALTO SAX

18th Century Irish Folksong

WHEN IRISH EYES ARE SMILING

ALTO SAX

Words by CHAUNCEY OLCOTT
and GEORGE GRAFF, JR.
Music by ERNEST R. BALL

THE WILD COLONIAL BOY

ALTO SAX

Traditional

Moderately

WILD ROVER

ALTO SAX

Traditional